Learning to Read, Step by Step!

Ready to Read   **Preschool–Kindergarten**
• big type and easy words • rhyme and rhythm • picture clues
For children who know the alphabet and are eager to begin reading.

Reading with Help   **Preschool–Grade 1**
• basic vocabulary • short sentences • simple stories
For children who recognize familiar words and sound out new words with help.

Reading on Your Own   **Grades 1–3**
• engaging characters • easy-to-follow plots • popular topics
For children who are ready to read on their own.

Reading Paragraphs   **Grades 2–3**
• challenging vocabulary • short paragraphs • exciting stories
For newly independent readers who read simple sentences with confidence.

Ready for Chapters   **Grades 2–4**
• chapters • longer paragraphs • full-color art
For children who want to take the plunge into chapter books but still like colorful pictures.

STEP INTO READING® is designed to give every child a successful reading experience. The grade levels are only guides; children will progress through the steps at their own speed, developing confidence in their reading.

Remember, a lifetime love of reading starts with a single step!

The editors would like to thank Jim Breheny, Director, Bronx Zoo, and EVP of WCS Zoos &
Aquarium, New York, for his assistance in the preparation of this book.

Wild Kratts is a Kratt Brothers Company/9 Story Entertainment production
© 2013 WK3 Productions Inc.

Step into Reading, Random House, and the Random House colophon are registered
trademarks of Penguin Random House LLC.

Visit us on the Web!
StepIntoReading.com
randomhousekids.com

Educators and librarians, for a variety of teaching tools, visit us at
RHTeachersLibrarians.com

ISBN 978-1-101-93171-4 (trade) — ISBN 978-1-101-93172-1 (lib. bdg.) —
ISBN 978-1-101-93173-8 (ebook)

Printed in the United States of America
10 9 8 7 6 5 4 3 2 1

Wild Animal Babies!

by Martin Kratt and Chris Kratt

Random House 🏠 New York

Hey, it's us,
the Kratt Brothers.
I'm Martin.
And I'm Chris.

We love learning about
the Creature Powers
of different animals—
especially baby animals!

Animal babies
aren't just cute.
They play and practice
every day to learn
about their amazing
Creature Powers!

Let's go meet some of our favorite baby animals in the wild!

Giant Pandas!

Stuffo has to learn
how to eat bamboo.
He practices holding it
with a thumb-like pad
while he chews.

"Thanks for the hug,
Stuffo," says Martin.

Zebras!

Zebra babies like Maze are called foals.

Maze was ready to run on the day she was born.

"And here's why!"

Chris shouts.

"Hungry lions are coming!

Let's get out of here fast!"

Orangutans!

Orangutan babies have
strong feet and hands.
They spend most of
their lives in the trees.
They have to hang on tight.

"You have quite a grip!"

says Chris.

Cheetahs!

Spotswat learns to climb
with his mom
to get a better look around.
Cheetahs watch out
for dinner—and danger!

A cheetah cub's favorite
game is chase!
When Spotswat grows up,
he will have to hunt
for his own dinner.

Sea Otters!

Sea otter pups learn to float when they are very little. Cork can also take a rest on his mom's belly.

Cork is a good swimmer.
His thick fur keeps him
warm in the cold water.

Spider Monkeys!

Grabsy is learning
a special kind of swinging
called brachiation.
She moves hand over hand
through the trees.

Spider monkeys can
swing very fast!
"Go, Grabsy, go!"
shout the brothers.

Wolves!

Howler made his first howl
when he was six weeks old.
Howling helps a wolf pack
talk to each other
and stay together.

Arrrrhoooooo!
"I hear you howling,"
Martin tells Chris.

Ring-Tailed Lemurs!

Clingon rides on
her mom's back
while she is young.
She has to hold on tight.

Mom runs and jumps
from tree to tree.
She takes care of Clingon
until she can survive
on her own.

Our animal friends play
to practice their special
Creature Powers.
What Creature Power
will you practice today?